SENSING TRANSFORMATION
Poetic Reflections

SENSING

TRANSFORMATION

Poetic Reflections

BROTHER EUGENE GIZZI, C.F.A.

 Alexian Publications Group *2004*

AN ALEXIAN DOVE ARTS BOOK
PUBLISHED BY ALEXIAN PUBLICATIONS GROUP

Published by Alexian Publications Group – Alexian Brothers Health System
3040 Salt Creek Lane
Arlington Heights, IL 60005

Illustration and Photography
Illustration of trees on cover and title page, all interior illustrations except
section dividers, and all interior photographs except page iii courtesy of
Brother Eugene Gizzi. Reproduction of oil painting on page 47 by Alexian
Brother Raphael created expressly for the poem Guardian Angel in 1963.
Portrait of Brother Eugene Gizzi on page iii by Marc Hauser Photography,
Chicago, Illinois.

Design: ROJO Design, Chicago, IL
Editing: Alexian Publications Group

Published August, 2004

First Edition – First Printing

This book is printed on acid-free paper. ⊚

ISBN 0-9753469-0-3

ACKNOWLEDGMENTS
I would like to thank Brother Lawrence Krueger, Brother Thomas Keusenkothen,
and Dean Grant for their support and encouragement. I would also like to
thank Mike Kearns, Tiffany Parke, and Hollis Bolton of Alexian Publications
Group for all of their assistance with this, my first book.

Printed in Canada

ALEXIAN BROTHERS MISSION STATEMENT
For more than seven hundred years, the Alexian Brothers have cared for
the sick, the aged, the poor and the dying. The basic Judeo-Christian beliefs
that inspired the founders of this Catholic religious congregation sustain its
ministry today. This heritage is espoused by the governance, management
and entire health care team throughout Alexian Brothers Health System in
their mutual commitment to promote the physical, mental, spiritual and
social well-being of all individuals served through the health care ministry.

www.alexianbrothers.org

ABOUT THE AUTHOR

Brother Eugene (Gene) Gizzi, C.F.A., was born in 1931 into an Italian immigrant family in Mishawaka, Indiana. In 1949 he became a member of the Immaculate Conception Province of the Alexian Brothers, a Catholic congregation of religious Brothers. For over 700 years, the Alexian Brothers have cared for the sick, the aged, the poor and the dying. Their mission and ministry of healing continues to this day.

Brother Gene is an alumnus of Central Catholic High School (1949) in South Bend, Indiana, and after he had studied to become an Alexian Brother he attended the Alexian Brothers School of Nursing (1955). He holds a bachelors degree in social science from DePaul University and a masters degree in social work from Loyola University (1972), both located in Chicago, Illinois. He also received certification as a Graphoanalyst (handwriting analyst) in 1975.

Brother Gene has ministered in various nursing service positions with the American Province of the Alexian Brothers, as well as in medical social work and pastoral care. He has held various roles and functions within the Alexian religious community, including several directorships, one of which was as the Vocation Director. He has also worked in the Alexian Formation Program with men preparing for their religious vows as Alexian Brothers. In 1955 he was one of five original Brothers assigned to Father Flanagan's Boys' Town to assist with healthcare, and in 1981 he was commissioned by the Alexian Brothers as the pioneer Brother for their Philippine Mission. Presently (since 1999) he is the Brother Visitor at St. Alexius Medical Center in Hoffman Estates, Illinois, an Alexian Brothers facility.

INTRODUCTION

While strolling through the woods during a November retreat in 1991, I saw a barren tree. It captivated me by its stark, stripped yet sturdy appearance; and introspectively I realized I was witnessing a reality of life: shedding of the old. Then I saw the breathtaking beauty of a dogwood tree with some of its buds starting to blossom, and the reality image was now complete: in life I shed the old and gradually take on the new.

Nature taught me a lesson that touches my inner self to this day. The two trees, one barren and the other starting to blossom forth, were visible reminders of the realities of life: we shed the old and take on the new. Like the trees, as time passes and we grow, mature, and finally die, we encounter a series of transitions in life that result in transformations for which we take responsibility. Yet, as we shed the old and take on the new, this newness does not come all at once; rather it comes on gradually, and life's process continues. That is a reality, and each transformation is beautiful in itself. The hope is that we can and do sense these transformations in body, mind and spirit, and thereby grow to become more of who we truly are, who we are called and meant to "Be," until our final transformation with God for eternity.

This experience also reinforced the growing need for reflection, meditation and quiet time in my life to better listen to and hear my inner self and my Higher Power, and share accordingly. Composing poems seemed to surface spontaneously from this blessed encounter with nature and from my ongoing ministry in health care, relating to the sick, dying, and their families and friends. The need to write my inner reflections on paper became a mission, as well as thera-peutic. During that retreat I was moved to sketch and paint both trees together, as the complement they were to each other, and titled the drawing "Sensing Transformation." Later I wrote a poem by the same title, and this became the trademark for my art and poetry works, "Sensing Transformation Cards by Geno." As a boy I was known as Geno.

A significant feature in many of my art forms is the butterfly, which is symbolic of transformation. From a little worm, which hibernates in the darkness of a cocoon and undergoes life's transitions, it bursts forth from the cocoon transformed into one of the most beautiful of God's creations, the butterfly. This masterpiece of beauty became an important reminder for me about the resurrection of Christ; and it dramatizes even more so another of nature's lessons about shedding the old and taking on the new. My encounter with nature, especially through the two trees, made for a memorable and awesome spiritual experience, which continues to this day.

My poems seem to find meaning in the lives of some people, who in turn have continually encouraged me to publish them. It took many years of their urging for me to finally take the step. My sister, Virginia Zellers, has been my biggest promoter, as sisters will be, and so too my brother, Guy Gizzi. I thank them both with all my heart. Thanks also to friends, who continually and even persistently urged me to "do something about your poems, so people can read and benefit from them." To them I acknowledge the importance of their kind probing; and my gratitude also goes to Arvena Morgan and Sister Jacinta Diebold, O.S.F., who were dedicated probers. A most important acknowledgement must be given to one special friend who personally visited and talked to me about the importance of publishing. She was the major motivator who finally convinced me to make a concerted effort, which led to this finished product. For permission from my Congregation of Alexian Brothers to pursue this publication I am blessed and grateful. I am thankful for the wise recommendations by Brother Jeffrey Callander. Words cannot express my indebtedness in my journey to make this book an instrument of healing.

Some of the poems have an art piece, which at the time I felt compelled to create to complement the message conveyed. The artistic use of the butterfly throughout is a recall of the wonders of transformation, the beauty of all creation, and the uniqueness of each of us in the eyes of our creator and it has always been the symbolic reflection in my poems, my art, my life.

Finally, my appreciation, respect and gratitude reaches out to you, the readers, for allowing me the opportunity and privilege to enter your lives and share with you. May these reflections be of some comfort, encouragement, consolation, amusement, or simply thought provoking, and may they be helpful in a special manner for those persons in need of support and recovery. May they enable you to become aware of the blessings of "Sensing Transformation" in your lives and strive to become more of whom you are. And be assured, this entire endeavor—from poetically composing my thoughts to sharing them—has been and continues to be a growth and healing experience for me, and I am forever grateful and blessed.

Brother Gene

Eugene (Gene) Gizzi, C.F.A.

DEDICATION

I dedicate this book in loving memory of my mother,
CARMINA GIZZI,
in gratitude for all she was to me.

DEDICATION

GRATIA, MAMA *Thank you, Mama*

Mama said I came to them one February day,
In a suitcase the doctor carried
                    passing by their way.

Sounded strange to me, but that's what mama said;
And when the doctor took me out,
                    a cord was caught around my head.

My eyes grew large, as I listened to the outcome;
Ma said my head was blue, they pulled me out,
                    and that's where I came from.

In a suitcase? From the doctor?
                    Struggling with a cord about my neck?
The suitcase was mama's, I'm told;
                    confusing, but what the heck!

I was ok and that was important, putting
                    mama and papa in a state of awe,
When my color cleared, I started to cry,
                    a beautiful baby boy they saw.

Elation surfaces within me, as I recall mama's story;
The look of love she still gives me
                    and no longer needs to worry.

Oh, that Mother's Love I treasure,
                    as synonymous with my birth;
And that suitcase analogy for me as a child
                    is a precious memory of worth.

I'm grown up now, Mama, at least I like to think so;
And I thank you and papa for making me,
                    your, "Geno," from head to toe.

I'll always try to make you proud and
                    take care of that cord-entwined head
By confronting the darknesses of life, and
                    enabling the Spirit of Light instead.

Each birthday I grow wiser, and spend some quiet time alone,
And think of Mama's suitcase, the gift of life,
                    and the blessings of a home.

Gratia, Mama mia, for you and Papa making me;
From God, through you, a personification of your love
                    I came to be.

Mama, Mama, you live on forever in me;
What a consolation, knowing you're in heaven,
                    And I'm forever part of thee.

*Carmina, Emilio, Serge
Virginia, Eugene Gizzi*

*Brother Gene (bottom right) with
immediate family, 1936*

February 1996

CONTENTS

I

Life's Special Moments

SENSING TRANSFORMATION

In life it is strength we need to strive in our journey here on earth.
We search for the ways to grow
and be someone indeed of worth.

Let us learn from each experience and come our "Self" to know.
Only then can we shed the old
and the gift of newness show.

It is a matter of awakening; it is a matter of re-creation.
And as Self-knowledge takes its hold,
it is a sensing transformation.

As the tree becomes barren and some even must die,
Just beyond it can be seen
a live tree catching the eye.

As my old "Self" must die, yet remain always a part of "Me,"
Seek that awareness to enable a rebirth
in and with the universe come to be.

Slowly and surely the blossoms will appear,
Just as the gift of Love in all humankind
will transform me year by year.

Yes, it is a matter of awakening; it is a matter of re-creation.
And as Self-knowledge takes it hold,
it is a sensing transformation.

Grow each day to become more of who you are.

1993

A CONNECTION

I saw a leaf falling from a tree,
  Which bore it, nourished it,
    Enabled it to grow and be.

The beauty of its colors could be seen,
  Which revealed its plant-life cycle,
    Unique in this universe supreme.

The leaf was part of a family tree,
  Which took its place amongst the others,
    Yet a separation was meant to be.

It fell from the branch at its given time,
  Which sent a message to us all,
    Revealing a transition with its Autumn sign.

Each leaf has a life cycle of its very own,
  Which does our Creator touch,
    Blending with nature's design, never alone.

I saved this leaf so beautiful and free,
  Which attracted me immediately.
    I felt a special connection:
      This leaf was a reflection of me.

September 2001

A SCENIC PSALM

Calm blue water as far as the eye can see.
Waves playing in sight, rhythmical and carefree.
Beauty, tranquility and healing as meant to be;
Yet a mystery lies within this scene captivating me.

"Not a care in the world!" fills my mind,
As I scan each feature of this awesome design.
There can be no other; it's one of a kind,
And it found me here at this place and time.

A long breath in; a long breath out.
Relax. I see a sailboat floating about.
The colors of the sails seem to shout,
That it's one of this picturesque privileged lot.

Now a cruiser speeds by, as if to disrupt the calm;
Instead it adds to the sacredness of this scenic psalm.
Each new etching adds its colors and sound,
That the Creator blends into nature's crown.

Huge rocks are settled along the coast,
Made to order for sitting, resting, and visualizing the most.
Warm sand, smooth stones, and tree branches lifted to toast
And compliment the scene, and innocently boast.

Fresh air with a breeze just right.
Birds in the sky, an inspirational sight,
Flying freely, oblivious of any earthy plight.
And suddenly a childish image: me riding high on a kite.

I see more birds above.
There and there a beautiful white dove
In the grandeur of the sky, clouds, sun; and there, a plane above.
My heart overflows with the sensuousness of love.

I'm experiencing a miracle with a lesson to learn:
Many came, saw, learned before me; it's now my turn
To witness nature's elements and our relationship confirm,
And any conflicts between us brought to term.

What's this I feel on my cheek? A tear –
For the privilege of seeing God's signature in nature so near and clear,
And a prayerful plea that this beauty we never smear
To continue nature's revelation to all humankind, that God is here.

October 2003

II

Life is a Series of Transitions

FREEDOM – RESPONSIBILITY

How important it is for me
  to become who "I" am;
To journey in this universe
  and thereby take a stand.

It has nothing to do with
  selfishness or vanity or power;
It is not the desire to dominate
  or stand constant on a tower.

Rather it is a matter of Freedom to my person
  – independently "Me" and unique;
And the Responsibility that goes with "Me,"
  rather than elsewhere seek.

Life is filled with mystery
  and one never travels it alone;
As we learn and grow, toil and sow,
  with others we make our home.

The colors of our life shine forth,
  touching somehow all humankind;
And as we walk upon this earth,
  our footprints make its sign.

Freedom is revealed by the color
  of life we each possess;
Responsibility guides our footprints,
  meeting others and doing our best.

That's the way it is with
  this given life we live;
Freedom – Responsibility are gifts,
  we must always strive to give.

1994

BLESSED TRANSFORMATION

Life is a series of transitions,
    which on our "Person" changes are imposed.
It's reality of life with its ups and downs,
    effecting us, then holistically transposed.

Spiritual, social, emotional, intellectual, physical
    – five aspects of our "Being;"
And when chipped at during life's journey,
    transformations occur, giving our character new meaning.

Known or unknown, accepted or not,
    without permission changes often occur.
Personality and character are effected,
    thereby behavior and actions for sure.

Whether transformations are imposed or not,
    I truly remain "Me;"
And with self-knowledge my holistic "Self"
    becomes clearer with a vision to be free.

Transitions to transformations
    is the pattern of life for us all;
Though pains of humanness are always present,
    A blessed life is our constant Call.

The decision is ours, as we come to know
    the influences in our life.
The choice is ours with spiritual aids
    for Blessed Transformations during our earthly strife.

August 1995

LONELY IN THE SHADOW

I find myself so lonely in the shadow of the sun,
And I ask myself, "Why? What is it that I've done?"
The days are short; the nights are long.
Work seems to drag, and nowhere a song.
Sleep, doze, yawn are signs of my desire;
Liveliness is stilted and motivation lacks its fire.
I want to sit and let it all pass away;
Turn to God and others, but don't know what to say.

It's a dark night of the soul, I hear it said;
Yet I'm too tired, it seems, for that route to tread.
With energy low, vision blurred, and God hard to find,
"I don't care" rings loud and clear and tends to be a bind.
There are ups and downs in these days, however,
Giving me hope; yet fear it will last forever.
"Look with myself," I hear my heart say;
Yet I avoid this lest a trick my mind play.

I know enough that this is not the way to be.
I don't want the shadow, rather the sun to thereby see.
But like it or not, I know down deep
To check my shadow-side will find what I seek.
The problem lies in my not wanting to know;
And so I do not seek, rather avoid and not show.
So lonely in the shadow; yet so safe somehow,
Maintaining a mask and isolation allow.

Oh, so weary and my heart wants to cry.
I look around, breathe shallow and only sigh.
There's a flicker of hope in the tunnel of darkness;
I reach out for it in a weak attempt to harness.
Yet shoulders and back start to slump,
And every action of the day seems to cause a bump;
Till my mind, heart and body are so weak and frail,
And although heaven surrounds me, the feeling is hell.

I cannot, will not, stay this way:
A victim of illusions and to all things fallen prey.
Life is worth living and strength can be had
In the place of chronic apathy and always feeling sad.
Laughter, happiness, companionship, love are there;
Yet anger, resentment, self-pity hover the air.
I need help. I want help, a way to set me free;
Yet I stay alone in the shadow, and help I cannot see.

Strange, I know what is happening and feel the pain.
I know the path that will make me sane.
I know the wonders of a healthy body and mind.
I know God's grace renders a blessed sign.
I know I can stand strong and rise above it.
I know to my Higher Power I must submit.
I know it's my responsibility and my choice to make:
Lonely in my shadow
                    or sunshine for my sake.

1994

These reflections surfaced when ministering to people
who felt their lives were hopeless, as I witnessed their
struggles to overcome their difficulties.

LOVE IS...

Forgiving. For giving.
    Never thought of that before.
The word is one, yet also two,
    and hits right to the core.

Love in the heart is for giving;
    yet in the world it can also be skewed.
        All around us we witness hoarding
        and people in constant feud.

This virtue of love is basic to all,
    given by our Life-Source Supreme.
        And it's meant to be healing;
            It's not a fantasy or dream.

Love. We know it. We show it.
      We want it. We abuse it.
          We need it. We fear it.
          We treasure it. We share it.
Yet mixed feelings and emotions
    become aroused by love
And too often love is stifled,
    never surfacing above.

Love is Understanding – to see, learn, grow.
Love is Compassion – empathy show.
Love is Forgiving – our "Self" humbly know.

Reach within yourself,
      where love dwells in the heart.
Now, touch it, use it, "Be" it –
      make a start.

Then your "Self" will become enflamed
      with a forgiving energy thrust,
Spilling out to be for giving to others
      with a healing trust.

In that way, all the colors of your heart
      in radiant beauty will show
With Understanding and Compassion
      through your hands to others a constant flow.

Then, too, each day will be a blessed reminder
      amongst the living,
That love is forgiving
      and also for giving.

January 1995

A ROSE AND MAN

The beauty of a rose – its scent, color and varied kind
Is like the beauty of man – with scent, color and wonders of a mind.

Rose petals open gradually, each a delicate twist and curve,
Like the physical features of man's body carved out to serve.

One is attracted to the rose by the vision it renders of warmth and love,
As the person of man reveals the healing, loving Creator above.

The petals will fall, the color will fade; yet a rose is a rose
                                        and special we know.
Man's body weakens, features fade; yet a man is a man
                                        and special, God told us so.

A rose is one image of God's beauty and Love, and reminds us a
                                        Higher Power is in control.
A man is made to the image of God, and reflects His wonders in
                                        gifts of body and soul.

Both so different, yet so much alike, placed here in earth's design;
Both fulfill their purpose, when a rose and a man each other find.

May 1996

14

BRIGHT SIDE OF LIFE

Look at the bright side of life,
    Though there's always a dark side in our daily strife.
Unfortunately, some of us got programmed to live in the dark,
    And life's journey may fall short of a cherished landmark.

Look at life's bright side; we can learn it you know,
    Just like the dark side we learned was so.
There's the light and the dark, the ups and the downs, the good and the bad;
    To have a chronic dark, down, bad outlook is very sad.

Our Creator made all things good, including "Me;"
    Due to past circumstances for some this is hard to see.
It can be a matter of positive affirmations we need;
    Our task then is to open up and enable planting that positive seed.

What a shame that the traumas of life take such a toll,
    Dimming one's aura instead of letting it glow.
An even greater shame is our knowing better; yet living content
    In the dim dark side of life, rejecting the graces our Creator sent.

One grace is – looking at the bright side of life,
    Surfacing our gifts, talents, uniqueness during our earthly strife,
And not hiding the lamp of our "Being," rather letting it shine;
    Then we'll reflect good onto others, and others will reflect back in kind.

March 2002

I'LL HUMBLY COMPLY

What if I should die tonight?
What if I should die tonight?
What will I say to God
　　About my earthly plight?

There's a fear I have although unfounded.
There's a hold I have on life, humanly grounded.
There's anxiety about the unknown,
　　That makes my fear compounded.

A recall of my life takes center stage,
A recall of my actions to this present age.
A recall that highlights my life's blessings
　　And spiritual advantage.

Do I love God above all as I should?
Do I love my neighbor as myself the way I could?
Do I use my gifts and talents
　　For God's greater Good?

Tears come to my eyes, as I struggle to understand.
Tears blur the images of my life long plan.
Tears plead to God to forgive my sins, excuse my faults,
　　And before Him humbly stand.

The reality of my humanness puts up an earthly fight.
The blessings of my spirituality render grace-filled light.
The Healing Presence of God touches me
      And makes all things right.

Thanks God for the privilege of being one of Your creations.
Thanks God for the life-long blessings of human sensations.
Thanks God for this awareness of the reality
      Of life's transformations.

"I am the Resurrection and Life;
      He who believes in me shall never die."
I believe these words of Jesus,
      And with faith do not deny.
I let go and let God, and have faith in His Will;
      When He calls, I'll humbly comply.

July 2001

TAKE A GOOD LOOK

Life is full of surprises;
it's an old saying, you know.
        Don't believe it,
        just 'cause they say it's so.

Look around
at the activities of the day;
        See for yourself,
        people play, work, and pray.

Play and pray?
Work is high stress some authorities say.
        Then second comes lots of play,
        and trailing behind is time to pray.

Schedules, plans, double-shift,
rush home to family or a meal;
        The days so routine,
        stamped with a predictable seal.

Where are those surprises
they're always talking about?
        The perception is that life is
        "Happy-go-lucky," most tend to shout.

It's all there;
yes, right under your nose:
        Challenges each day brings,
        and secrets each of us knows.

We do our best and sometimes not
with ambivalence thrown in;
        We give and take, smile and frown,
        love and hate, and sometimes sin.

The roteness of our daily life
can really take its toll,
      And gradually a loss of
      creativity and soul.

The spontaneity, excitement and
spirituality start to drag,
      With emotional and physical well-being
      playing a fool's game of tag.

The challenge is to learn, grow, relate,
and make life a bit of heaven;
      Be healthy, happy, holy
      and forgive seventy times seven.

With a Higher Power and others on your side,
trust, have faith and you can't fail.
      Just don't settle for less
      and let it all go to hell.

Yes, life is full of surprises,
take a good look and study it well,
      Before the surprise you find is
      that you've put your life up for sale.
Then you discover it is "Happy-go-lucky," alright,
      because the difference
      is hard to tell.

June 1996

WHO AM I?

"Who are you?" came this confronting question,
That triggered from within myself, "Who am I?"
Name, age and address was my spontaneous suggestion;
When asked again, my job, education, vocation was my reply.

"These are things you acquired, but who are you?"
I sat stunned and dumb for what to say.
I searched within for an answer that's true;
My heart beat fast and my mind whirled in a strange way.

I always thought of myself by what people know and see of me,
Those physical aspects of my life to date.
I never considered them acquisitions that would come to be
Physical forces controlling my personal fate.

Too often we live behind the mask
Of what we've acquired and so too live;
It takes its toll and demands the task
Of undoing the projected images we give.

There are two levels of my "Being": physical and spiritual.
The physical can easily overwhelm and smother;
And the spiritual becomes a mere ritual,
When in fact as important as the other.

That question that beckons a statement
About who I am and much more,
Prompts a personal journey for enlightenment;
Although I never gave it much thought before.

I'm never too old to seek and learn
The who, when, what, where, and why's about me.
Truthfully, it's something for which I yearn –
To become more of whom I'm meant to "Be."

March 2003

20

AWAKE, IT'S TIME

In the deep recess of my mind
    I wonder round and what to find.
Asleep somehow during this inward journey,
    brushing all aside in a flurry.

It's dark in there, yet so clear somehow,
    like the keen sight of the sentinel owl.
See it all, yet excuse it 'cause it's dark;
    aware of its presence, it made its mark.

Is this a dream? Am I conscious now?
    Through tough soil I seem to plow.
Yet I struggle along and in the distance a song;
    I hear it and know now, it won't be long.

Awake, awake, it's time to live,
    time to work, play, receive and give!
Awake, awake, come now at last,
    the world around is passing fast!

I may want to sleep and let sameness be so;
    that's a reality down deep I know.
Yet, being awake and coming to see
    brings awareness and understanding
    and a response to truly "Be."

October 1995

III

Life is a Journey of Learning and Growth

THE AURA SURROUNDING US

Awake to the beauty of all creation
With appreciation and respect through each sensation.
        Acknowledge gifts and talents we possess,
        As well as omissions we humbly confess.
Enable each gift and talent to ever shine forth
And follow their God given course.
        Know that Love is the supreme gift of all,
        There for the giving at each beckon call.

Witness and experience healing power abound
In the aura surrounding us found.
        The colors of your spectrum radiate and glow,
        Just as a butterfly's beauty attracts us so.
It's time. Be ready. The glory of God is here.
Activate the Spirit of Love within and have no fear.
        Purity and Peace at birth is our legacy;
        Sharing that with others is what is meant to be.

April 2003

24

A NEW DAY

Wonderful is each new day, God made it especially for me;
And all He asks is an open heart to enter and with us be.

What wonders God grants us in our daily life;
Yet sometimes miss it in our encounters and strife.

Beauty of the universe, Companionship with others,
    The glory of the person I am,
Colors of the environment, Dynamics of all creatures
    From bird to beast, even the little clam.

Details of it all are known to God, our Maker and Supreme Holy One;
Each new day with its changes and wonders reveals God's creation is never done.

Its awesome beauty we may fail to see, how unfortunate that may be;
Since we partake in the balance of God's Design for all to know and see.

Oppressed and shadowed may be our case through unfounded self-glory;
Yet in unity with all God's creation evolves the mysterious and Divine Story.

What must we do to become more aware and fulfill our part in God's Call?
Just accept God's generous Love; He embraces you, the universe and all.

Then each day has greater meaning to meet the challenges that come our way,
Praising God in the glories of His creation
    – including me – and know the gift of a new day.

Listen now, and hear what God has to say,
    Through the wonders and privilege of another day.

October 1995

ROOTS IN HUMANITY

I look around and see the world
     in its wonder and glory;
I look around and see the world
     in its turmoil and sad story.
Such beauty, diversity and order
     is the universal case;
Yet disfigurement, shortage, chaos
     brings universal waste.

Where am I in the midst
     of these dynamic pulls?
Working, suffering, playing one
     of many worldly fools?
Looking forward, backward, up, down,
     sideways and all around,
I stand in the midst of my environment,
     and find pollution even in sound.

God created heaven and earth
     and each creature in it;
God created me too, with all humankind,
     in a universe designed to fit.
All is wonderful and grand;
     look and one can tell.
It's our human neglect that causes problems,
     putting the world up for sale.

I am made to the image and likeness of God
     to give honor and glory to Him,
To love my neighbor as myself
     and make effort to avoid sin.
With Faith in God and Hope in His grace,
     Love is the Counsel above all.
But "Where am I at?" is a question to answer
     in response to my God-given Call.

I am a person, unique
    and special some way
With roles, functions and prayer,
    including some time to play.
Together with fellow brothers and sisters
    of all humankind,
I have my place, according to God's Will
    in His Blessed Design.

"Peace on earth and Goodwill to all,"
    is the angels' message heard.
Care for the earth and creatures in it,
    is what I must continually learn.
The universe is beautiful,
    and we strive to respect and maintain it indeed.
I am one helping creation in the midst of it all;
    I am a seed.

I am a SEED,
    planted in the soil of God's Design,
To grow, blossom and participate,
    maintaining God's creation
        and there for all to find –
That I am GOD'S SEED,
    sprouting roots in humanity,
        one seed amongst others,
            Each special, One of a kind.

July 1995

THE BUTTERFLY AND MAN

Awake to the beauty of all creation.
Awake to the wonders of each sensation.
    Awake to the new dawn, shaking fear and trepidation.
        Awake to the gift of life, assuring eternal salvation.

See colors that adorn earth, sea and sky.
See plants and rock formations, where they lie.
    See animals crawl and run, and birds fly.
        See human nature's complementary role apply.

Know the creature once a worm.
Know the cocoon, where it spent its term.
    Know the darkness that embraced the turn.
    Know the miracle of a butterfly it does confirm.

Like the butterfly we were infants destined to grow.
Like the butterfly we encountered each developmental toll.
    Like the butterfly we have dark nights of the soul.
    Like the butterfly we can a miracle know.

The butterfly and man, both experience transitions.
The butterfly and man, both reveal blessed transformations.
    The butterfly and man, both wonders of life's sensations.
    The butterfly and man, both miracles of God's creations.

Wake up! Be aware of the butterfly, unique, tender and beautiful.
Wake up! Be aware that man is likewise, and sent to be fruitful.
    Wake up! Know that life is a gift and wonderful.
    Wake up! Know that we are touched by God and Special.

Arise! To His image and likeness God made us so.
Arise! To life's journey and God's revelations come to know.
    Arise! It's time to see, learn and continue to grow.
    Arise! It's time to be thankful and our gratitude show.

June 2003

WITHOUT A SOUND

There's a strange sensation in my gut;
       what it is I know.
On the outside all is calm;
       inner emotions do not show.

My heart beats stronger;
       breathing is faster now.
A tingling felt in my arms and hands;
       general malaise is grasping me somehow.

I sit still and quiet,
       lifting my heart and mind;
Yet the dark night of my soul
       is an obvious undesirable sign.

A blankness holds me captive
       at sporadic moments of the day;
Like a therapeutic escape,
       caught immobile between work and play.

A period of rest I welcome,
       but blankness, "Please, No."
Rest is beneficial,
       but in blankness I'm trapped with nowhere to go.

I shut my eyes;
       I see the snow of a TV screen.
I sink deeper;
       without a sound I hear myself scream.

Yes, a reflection on isolation
       does each of us well,
Because buying the darkness of isolation,
       may put my life up for sale.

January 1998

IV

Life Celebrates Special Days
for Remembrance

THE MESSAGE OF CHRISTMAS

"Peace on earth; Goodwill to all,"
    the message of Christmas we know.
Christ was born to save us all,
    because He loved us so.

This Holiday we celebrate with plenty
    of gifts, food, parties and friends;
But let's not forget to include in it all
    – love – the true spirit that Christmas sends.

The Peace in Love brings calm and ease;
    it renders light in the time of need.
The Goodwill in Love brings joy and praise
    and understanding, a constant plead.

The earth will feel this healing spirit,
    as Peace and Goodwill touches all;
Then each person and element of God's creation
    will come to know Love's Call.

Peace, Goodwill – how will it come to be
    to fulfill the Christmas purpose of Love?
Let each of us strive to become who we truly are
    with unique gifts and talents from above.

Then reach out with unity in diversity
  and together one and all stand tall,
Singing and living the song of the angels on high,
  "Peace on earth; Goodwill to all."

That's the message of Christmas,
  the blessed gift we received and know;
Peace, Goodwill, Love – Christ came
  and lived on earth for this to show.

Now we are the messengers of this wondrous gift,
  that we receive and also give;
And we take the responsibility to pass it on,
  making this our world a better place to live.

December 1995

ALLELUIA

ALLELUIA, the Lord is risen
and brought salvation to us all.
Through His life and death
we come to find our special
earthly Call.

He won victory over death;
through all darkness
His glory shines.
We render Him praise, now and always,
as Savior of all times.

May the blossoms of your "Being"
take root,
burst forth,
and before the world grow.
Through the Words our Savior taught us,
let our life His lessons show.

Then Easter will be fulfilled indeed,
ever revealed in you and me
With the Spirit of the Risen Christ
seen in the beauty,
colors,
uniqueness
each of us is called to be.

Happy Easter!   And may it continue to be
a blessed transformation.

March 1995

ON YOUR WEDDING DAY

Life is so beautiful; nature shows in its array.
May your lives be special too,
              As the beauty of your Wedding Day.

Your vow is Oneness, Commitment and Love,
An awesome Blessing from the Father above.

In your Oneness find a bonding,
              And strength from your Commitment;
And with Love is faith and trust in each other
              To grow and complement.

Life is so beautiful; nature shows in its array.
May your lives grow in beauty
              From the time "I do" you vowed
                    on your Wedding Day.

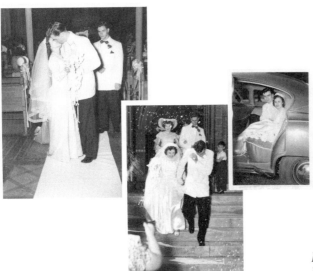

Wedding
Darrell and Virginia
Zellers
St. Joseph Church
Mishawaka, In.
July 22, 1950

Brother Gene's sister and her
husband on their wedding day

1992

V.

Life is a Passage

AGING WILL COME

"No one cares," the old man said,
His face all wrinkled, no hair on his head;
Marks here and there, his sensitive skin bled.

"I'm so alone," the old woman cried,
Head and eyes low, tears flow as she sighed;
"I did the best I could. I tried. I tried."

He shuffled slowly in his attempt to walk.
She turned her head as she began to talk.
Both avoided those who may want to gawk.

Each strives for dignity to maintain,
Remembering some basics to appear sane,
Eating carefully to avoid any stain.

Yet their demeanors grow frail, unsteady and slow,
Their eyes lose much of that radiance and glow,
Their memories grasp for what they used to know.

This image of some Aged persons may be true,
Even a reality in our own family too;
And a voice within me says, "Could this some day be you?"

Reach out and open up your heart.
Lift up your prayers, remain healthy and smart.
Become informed and a Concerned Presence as a start.

Then health, happiness and holiness find
By following the Golden Rule sublime,
And taking one day at a time
      Remembering that aging will come;
      It's God's will, not yours nor mine.

May 1997

THE MIRACLE OF AGING

What a gift it is to reminisce
      the wonders of the past,
To realize and acknowledge
      the saying, "Time passes fast."

Only the miracle of aging
      can boast of this fair gift;
When accepted by the Aged and the Young,
      each phase of life is rendered a lift.

Oh, we the children of many years experience,
      who worked, struggled, built, restored,
      nourished the environment,
      as we gave birth to precious life;
Take heart in knowing that
      our labors, laughter, tears, success,
      sickness, prayers, death and journey
      fortifies each new generation's earthly strife.

We see in our youth our own transition,
      since we are the image for their reflection;
Our gift of experiences and wisdom
      cloaks them with knowledge and protection.

Life is a dedication and a commitment
      to self and all humankind;
The imprint we make through our life stories
      in our young ones, we are sure to find.

Yes, indeed, what a gift it is to reminisce
      the wonders of our past,
To realize and acknowledge
      "Time passes fast."
We share that time and all it contains
      – to be passed on and forever last.

1999

BE REFRESHED

Laugh at yourself.
Come on,
go ahead.
Life's too short;
be refreshed
With a Sense of Humor instead.

There's a time to be serious.
Come on,
it's a fact.
Life's too short;
be refreshed
With a Sense of Humor in the act.

There can be both.
Come on,
balance up a bit.
Life's too short;
be refreshed
With a Sense of Humor one with the
other will fit.

There is harmony,
when both merge.
Come on,
it's the healthy way to live.
Life's too short;
be refreshed
With a Sense of Humor the true beauty
of your "Being" will be revealed
and to others give.

April 1998

AGING: IT'S A REALITY

What is it that I desire? The thought runs wild these days.
What is in store for me? As life's journey runs its earthly maze.
What do I see ahead? An array of colors, dreams and shades of grays.
What do I really need? Now that's a question to be humbly and honestly raised.

Then let's get with it. – What do you say?
Let's make a start. – Set a time for specifics during each day.
And that means – A balance of prayer, work and play.
It's time to start. – We hear that only too often; yet confronted with chronic delay.

You might begin – by becoming simply aware.
You have five senses – see, hear, taste, smell, and feel even the air.
You need people – for relationships, growth and the need to share.
You have a Higher Power – so, know God is always there.

"Ask and you shall receive" – resources that are credible.
"Knock and it shall be opened" – discipline and persistence make it possible.
"Search and you shall find" – ways and means that are available.
Remember this prayer formula? – It makes Enlightenment attainable.

With a positive attitude – healing comes at last.
So, stop – and relax.
Set your mind – to the task.
Get help – for the facts.

You know what I think is the FACT? The Reality of AGING crept in.
Aging – from birth, infancy, childhood, adolescence, adulthood, old age
        and on to eternity win.
You want the TRUTH? That's it; and with this awareness and acceptance
        of aging a new phase of life can begin.
It's a REALITY. It's part of life… so lighten up
        with a chuckle or two and a hearty grin.

October 2000

VI.

Life is Touched by
a Spiritual Awareness

CROWN OF LIFE
James 1:1–12

A meditation on this passage.

Trials and tribulations.
O God, why must it be this way?
    I hear Jesus answer:
    I have a plan for you;
        Hear what I have to say.

Count it as pure joy, as best you can,
When involved with many trials;
    Thereby Faith is tested
    And Endurance nourished
        Throughout life's miles.

With Endurance perfected
Maturity of person sets in,
    Lacking in nothing;
    Rather battles of life to win.

Grant us Wisdom, O Lord,
You give it generously to all.
    We need only ask with doubtless faith,
    When to You, we turn and call.

The doubter is like the turf
Tossing here, there, everywhere;
    Devious and erratic in all that he does,
    The fabric of his life begins to tear.

In Humility and Love confront the circumstances
Of lowliness and scorn in earthly strife.
    Happy the man who holds out to the end through trials;
    Once proved, he will receive the crown of life.

March 1998

VALUES OF LOVE

My Higher Power gave me a gift,
    a gift not meant to keep;
So many persons I encounter,
    that gift is what they seek.

It's there within each of us,
    waiting for release;
And it's replaced with a
    grace-filled satisfaction and peace.

At times the frailties
    of our humanness take hold;
Thereby the danger of
    our precious gift being cheaply sold.

That gift is LOVE
    for all to know and see;
Love is the purpose
    our Creator made each of us to "Be."

The heart is not large enough
    to hold all the Love it ban contain;
It spills over,
    touching others to love the same.

Compassion,
    Dignity,
        Holism,
            Collaboration,
                Care of the Poor
    are Values of Love;

Put into action the Spirit is revealed
        and we are Healing Instruments
            of our Higher Power above.

December 1998

FAITH. HOPE. LOVE.

Faith

Let it be acclaimed.
It's the Wisdom in the mystery
   of God, that many people proclaim.
Release it, like taking
   a step into the unknown;
It's then with each step forward, your path is shown.
Faith – that gift and virtue that is a must.
Faith – my expression of confidence and trust.

Hope

Let it shine.
It's the light in the darkness,
   rendering solace sublime.
Release it, like an
   anchor in the bay;
It's then you have courage to endure the way.
Hope – that virtue that sparks my "Being."
Hope – my way of seeing.

Love

Take it in.
It's always been there,
   not just a prize to win.
Release it, like the
   freedom of a bird;
It's then, your "person" is truly heard.
Love – the greatest virtue of them all.
Love – our true "Call."

Faith, Hope, Love

And the greatest of these is Love –
   Words from God above.

May 1995

46

MY GUARDIAN ANGEL

*"To his angels he has given command about you,
that they guard you in all your ways."*

Dear angel sent me from above
    Please guide me through the day
Hold tight my hand and help me love
    My Savior as I pray.

My thoughts and words so purify
    My actions make so kind
And lead me so that when I die
    My Savior I will find.

O angel, it is good to know
    Your presence day and night
And when through perils I must go
    Have crosses rendered light.

Forever will I thank you for
    Your guidance till the end
And I will try a little more
    To thank God for my friend.

Psalm 91

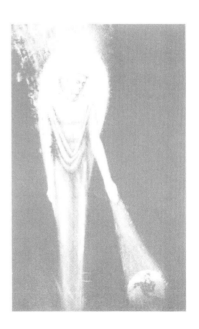

1957

VII.

Life is Worth Living,
Enjoy and be Happy!

MY FRIEND

A wonderful feeling it was to see you once again,
    And reaffirm in heart and mind you are indeed my friend.
Passage of time and changes take place in you and me alike,
    Yet our interior is of essence to always keep in sight.

Strange how on exteriors we tend to focus hard,
    Trying to make our body parts never retard.
Yet hair grays, heads bald, skin starts to wrinkle,
    We slow down a bit, have an ailment or two
    – yet our eyes still hopefully twinkle.

With time and age we pray that maturity takes true hold,
    And comes to learn and live the many lessons we've been told.
"To love God and neighbor as myself" – the Great Lesson of the Golden Rule,
    And as God's children we rise and fall using this Blessed Tool.

Accept me, dear friend, with my gifts, strengths, weaknesses as well.
    Let us continue to join minds and hearts in God's Love pray tell.
He made us to His likeness,
    So never on the dreary of life let us dwell.

Let us trust in God and have Faith and Hope;
    This will give us the graces we need to cope.
And in our fellow man God's Love can be found there too;
    Let's learn to know this, because their support can be so true.

What a blessing to know you, a gift in this life of mine.
   Thanks for being who you are to me – a Special Person so fine.
Though time may pass and distance even be the case,
   Prayer and spiritual connection knows no boundaries in time and space.

Yes, what a wonderful feeling it was to see you once again,
   And reaffirm in heart and mind that you are indeed my friend.
Yes, you are indeed my Friend.

Brother Gene with his
friend Andy Mendonsa
and Andy's children

1994

LAUGH IT OFF

The greatest grace I think sometimes
    Is the grace to laugh at yourself.
The fast pace, abundance of work,
    Leaves us seemingly with a lack of help.
The mind hurries, the emotions flare,
    And stress can be felt at its height.
The weight of it all takes its toll,
    As we struggle and decide: fight or flight.

How serious we get from encounters
    That beset our body and mind,
Attacking subtly with its cunning airs
    And we're suddenly caught in a bind.
Then we settle for self-pity and wallow
    In the mire of low self-esteem,
Feeling an emptiness throughout our being,
    Letting out a silent scream.

What's happened to that grace of laughter?
    Especially at unfounded seriousness?
What's happened to common sense,
    That yells, "Hey, you, what's all the fuss?"
That mire can be like quicksand,
    Which sucks us down and smothers
All life's energies, dreams, goals,
    And separates ourselves from others.

Life is not a bed of roses;
    Who ever told us that anyway?
Life has its highs and lows
    And unexpected realities that come into play.
Life is beautiful, however, regardless of its
    Hardships and often physical and mental pain.
Life is God's gift to us, and
    With free will we can choose to remain sane.

Sounds so easy – well it's not,
　　Because our humanness can be weak at times;
And due to circumstances in our past
　　Our "person" may miss constructive signs.
But we must not despair,
　　Rather do our best and see
That each struggle is a lesson to learn and grow
　　to become a better "Me."

Many times our perceptions are off,
　　And what we think – is not really so.
Many times, when tempted by unfounded fear,
　　We could strive to humbly say, "No!"
Many times when we get so serious,
　　And we hardly know what to do –
Many times we could chuckle and have a good laugh,
　　Rather than stand in the mire and stew.

Bless us, Father, for we have sinned;
　　We failed today to grin.
Give us the grace to laugh it off
　　And a joyous smile to win.
What may be needed for most of us –
　　Is to forgive ourselves and love;
Then relax a bit and know God's in control
　　And will shower us with the grace of humor from above.

For this we pray. Amen.

Amen

January 2002

GOOD MORNING

Good morning, God. Good morning, world.
Thank you for another day...

To give my creator honor and glory
    Through everything I do and every word I say.
To participate with all creation
    In the wonders of God's design.
To become who God wants me to "Be"
    In His image and likeness, one of a kind.
To share as a co-creator
    In the glory of God's love.
To be an Instrument of Healing
    For God's Spirit from above.
To see, know and respond to my place
    In the masterpiece of God's creation.
To experience again each sound, taste,
    Smell, sight and touch sensation.
To know the blessings of God's love
    In everything on earth: animal; mineral; plant.
To learn and share in everything growing,
    To each other a complement.
To strive and become more of who I am
    Through the support of God's gifts on earth.
To journey each day and do my best
    With Jesus as my focus, always first.
To "let go and let God" be a mantra
    And balance my time for prayer, work and play.
To know God loves me and always will,
    Gives me the faith and courage to follow His Way.

Good morning, God. Good morning, world.
Thank you, thank you for another day.

August 2002

A Note on the Type

The text of the main body of this book was set in a computer version of International Typeface Corporation (ITC) Berkeley Oldstyle.

The ITC Berkeley Oldstyle font is based on the 1938 work of Frederic Goudy for the University of California Press, located at Berkeley. This digital font remake is drawn by Tony Stan. This font contains Goudy's Berkeley inspiration while referencing other Goudy font designs such as the Kennerley font, Goudy Oldstyle font, Deepdene font, and Booklet Oldstyle font. The ITC Berkeley Oldstyle font remains one of the most time-honored text fonts today.

Printed at Friesens, Altona, Manitoba, Canada.